ID0754829

The Little Book of Boris

Compiled by Iain Dale

HARRIMAN HOUSE LTD

3A Penns Road
Petersfield
Hampshire
GU32 2EW
GREAT BRITAIN

Tel: +44 (0)1730 233870
Fax: +44 (0)1730 233880
Email: enquiries@harriman-house.com
Website: www.harriman-house.com

First published in Great Britain in 2007

ISBN: 1-9056-4164-8
ISBN 13: 978-1905641-64-2

British Library Cataloguing in Publication Data
A CIP catalogue record for this book can be obtained from the British Library.

Printed and bound in Great Britain by the CPI Group 'Antony Rowe, Chippenham'

Illustrations courtesy of Hoby, www.hobycartoons.com

Foreword

There are few politicians who could genuinely be described as a phenomenon. Boris Johnson is one. His appearances on *Have I Got News For You* have propelled him into the political stratosphere, building him a fan base way beyond the confines of politics. Boris has star quality. He's loved by many, ridiculed by some, feared by others. His candidacy for the London mayoralty has seen him accused by his opponents of being a racist, crook, philanderer and much more besides. It's a measure of his cross-party popularity that the dirty tricks department have been deployed on him so early in the campaign.

My abiding memory of Boris was spending a day with him when I was campaigning as the Conservative Party candidate in North Norfolk. Boris kindly agreed to come and support my efforts to be an MP (which sadly failed!). I had heard terrible stories of him being late, or turning up on the wrong day, so when I answered the phone at ten to nine that morning, my heart was already in my mouth. I thought I'd cover every organizational base there was to cover, but oh no I hadn't. "Morning, old bean," chirruped Boris. "Nearly at the station now." As the train was due to depart for Norwich at 9a.m. I was already worried. "Where exactly are you, Boris?" I whimpered. "Just coming into Kings Cross now," came the rather worrying response. Why worrying? Well, he was supposed to be at Liverpool Street. I just about managed not to cry, and rapidly created Plan B. I got him on the train to King's

Lynn – a mere ninety minute drive from my home near North Walsham, and then of course a ninety minute drive back. Bearing in mind he was due to speak at a lunch for 150 people at 1p.m., things were not looking good. In the end we managed to go to the glass making factory, do an interview with North Norfolk Radio and conduct an interview with the local paper in the back of the car without too much trouble. However, it meant we were forty-five minutes late for the lunch. We walked into the room and I expected to be lynched. But they all stood and cheered, because frankly they had never expected him to be on time. "Good old Boris," they cried. Only Boris could have got away with it. Meanwhile, I slumped into my chair, a nervous wreck, thinking to myself, "Never again".

Boris gave an interview to *GQ* magazine recently where he mused about the fact that he knew that to be a serious politician he would have to make a choice between ambition and buffoonery. A few weeks later he threw his hat into the ring and announced he wanted to be the Conservative candidate for Mayor of London. There's no doubt he has the intellect and ability to do the job, but in the end he has got to be himself. If he loses his humorous edge, he won't have the same magnetic appeal across the political spectrum he enjoys now. He'll become just like any other politician. Boris, just be yourself.

Iain Dale
Tunbridge Wells, August 2007

The Words of Boris

"I advise you all very strongly – go for a run, get some exercise, and have a beautiful day."

Cornered by reporters asking about his affair after a morning run. 15 November 2004

"It is better to have a serious man being a buffoon than a buffoon pretending to be a serious man."

Andrew Gilligan, *Evening Standard*

"When I look at the streets of London I see a future for the planet, a model of co-operation and harmony between races and religions, in which barriers are broken down by tolerance, humour and respect – without giving way either to bigotry, or the petty balkanisation of the Race Relations industry."

July 2007

"For all his taste for comedy, he has done nothing as inherently comic as Mayor Livingstone's risible cultivation of the Venezuelan President, Hugo Chavez. It should be asked: who is the real 'joke candidate' here?"

The Spectator, 21 July 2007

"For 10 years we in the Tory Party have become used to Papua New Guinea-style orgies of cannibalism and chief-killing, and so it is with a happy amazement that we watch as the madness engulfs the Labour Party."

After apologising for any offence, Boris said he would be happy to "add Papua New Guinea to my global itinerary of apology".

"There seems no reason to behave respectfully towards that little old woman coming out of the Post Office if you feel that she belongs to a culture that is alien from your own... Why not piss against the wall if you feel that it is not really your wall, but part of a foreign country."

Lend Me Your Ears, p207

On the Liberal Democrats:

"The Lib Dems are not just empty. They are a void within a vacuum surrounded by a vast inanition."

"What's my view on drugs? I've forgotten my view on drugs."

During the campaign trail of the 2005 general election.

"I'm kicking off my diet with a cheeseburger — whatever Jamie Oliver says, McDonald's are incredibly nutritious and, as far as I can tell, crammed full of vital nutrients and rigid with goodness."

While campaigning at McDonald's in Botley, Oxford, May 2005

"Voting Tory will cause your wife to have bigger breasts and increase your chances of owning a BMW M3."

On 'Big Brother', *The Observer*, 20 June 2004:

"I didn't see it, but it sounds barbaric. It's become like cock-fighting: poor dumb brutes being set upon each other by conniving television producers."

Explaining why he quit after a week as a management consultant:

"Try as I might, I could not look at an overhead projection of a growth profit matrix, and stay conscious."

"There is one measurement I hesitate to mention, since the last time I did, I am told, the wife of the editor of *The Economist* cancelled her subscription to the *Daily Telegraph* in protest at my crass sexism. It is what is called the Tottometer, the Geiger counter that detects good-looking women. In 1997, I reported these were to be found in numbers at the Labour conference. Now – and this is not merely my own opinion – the Tories are fighting back in a big way."

The Spectator, 10 February 2001

"Yes, cannabis is dangerous, but no more than other perfectly legal drugs. It's time for a rethink, and the Tory party – the funkiest, most jiving party on Earth – is where it's happening."

Daily Telegraph, 12 July 2001

"I don't see why people are so snooty about Channel 5. It has some respectable documentaries about the Second World War. It also devotes considerable airtime to investigations into lap dancing, and other related and vital subjects."

Daily Telegraph, 14 March 2002

"She [Polly Toynbee] incarnates all the nannying, high-taxing, high-spending, schoolmarminess of Blair's Britain. She is the defender and friend of everyone whose non-job has ever been advertised in the *Guardian* appointments page, every gay and lesbian outreach worker, every clipboard-toter and pen-pusher and form-filler whose function has been generated by mindless regulation. Polly is the high priestess of our paranoid, mollycoddled, risk-averse, airbagged, booster-seated culture of political correctness and 'elf 'n' safety fascism."

Daily Telegraph, 23 November, 2006

"Nor do I propose to defend the right to talk on a mobile while driving a car, though I don't believe that is necessarily any more dangerous than the many other risky things that people do with their free hands while driving – nose-picking, reading the paper, studying the A-Z, beating the children, and so on."

1 August 2002

"We are confident in our story and will be fighting this all the way. I am very sorry that Alastair Campbell has taken this decision but I can see that he got his tits in the wringer."

On Alastair Campbell's negative reply to *The Spectator's* report that the Government had influence the Queen Mother's funeral arrangements. *The Herald*, 24 April 2002

On driving a Ferrari:

"I seemed to be averaging a speed of X and then the M3 opened up before me, a long quiet Bonneville flat stretch, and I am afraid it was as though the whole county of Hampshire was lying back and opening her well-bred legs to be ravished by the Italian stallion."

Life in the Fast Lane, p261

"I forgot that to rely on a train, in Blair's Britain, is to engage in a crapshoot with the devil."

Daily Telegraph, 3 July 2003

"A horse is a safer bet than the trains."

Daily Telegraph, 3 July 2003

"The dreadful truth is that when people come to see their MP, they have run out of better ideas."

Daily Telegraph, 18 September 2003

"As snow-jobs go, this beats the Himalayas... It is just flipping unbelievable. He is a mixture of Harry Houdini and a greased piglet. He is barely human in his elusiveness. Nailing Blair is like trying to pin jelly to a wall."

Reaction to the Hutton Report *Daily Telegraph*, 29 January 2004, p. 21.

"Alan Clark... Here was a man, just like the readers of *GQ, Esquire, Loaded* – all the reassurance-craving magazines that have sprouted in the last 10 years – who was endlessly fascinated by the various advantages and disappointments of his own gonads."

"How can somebody as fat as you get so many good-looking women to find you attractive?"

Ardal Conyngham, Belfast

"Some readers will no doubt say that a devil is inside me; and though my faith is a bit like Magic FM in the Chilterns, in that the signal comes and goes, I can only hope that isn't so."

Daily Telegraph, 4 March 2004

"If Amsterdam or Leningrad vie for the title of Venice of the North, then Venice – what compliment is high enough? Venice, with all her civilisation and ancient beauty, Venice with her addiction to curious aquatic means of transport, yes, my friends, Venice is the Henley of the South."

Daily Telegraph, 11 March 2004

"All the warning we had was a crackling of the alder branches that bend over the Exe, and the stag was upon us. I can see it now, stepping high in the water, eyes rolling, tongue protruding, foaming, antlers streaming bracken and leaves like the hat of some demented old woman, and behind it the sexual, high pitched yipping of the dogs. You never saw such a piteous or terrible sight…"

"Look the point is ... er, what is the point? It is a tough job but somebody has got to do it."

On being appointed Shadow Arts Minister, 7 May 2004

"I want now to reassure all smokers that in one way I am on their side. It is precisely my continued failure to take up smoking that leads me to oppose a ban on smoking in public places... Above all, a ban on smoking in public places substitutes the discretion of the state for the individual will, in a way that is morally sapping."

"My chances of being PM are about as good as the chances of finding Elvis on Mars, or my being reincarnated as an olive."

"You ask the questions", *The Independent*, 17 June 2004, p.7.

Asked "Admit it: you want to become prime minister, don't you?" by Amanda Findlay of Bolton.

"Tremendous, little short of superb. On cracking form."

Asked how he was feeling after being sacked as Shadow Arts Minister for having misled Michael Howard. *The Times*, 15 November 2004.

"Nothing excites compassion, in friend and foe alike, as much as the sight of you ker-splonked on the tarmac with your propeller buried six feet under."

On being sacked from the Tory front bench. *Daily Telegraph*, 2 December 2004.

"I'm making absolutely no comment...and no, I did not."

When asked if he intentionally misled Michael Howard, leader of the Conservative Party.

"My friends, as I have discovered myself, there are no disasters, only opportunities. And, indeed, opportunities for fresh disasters."

On being sacked from the Tory front bench. *Daily Telegraph*, 2 December 2004, p.26.

"If there is one thing wrong with us all these days, it is that we are so mollycoddled, airbagged and swaddled with regulations and protections that we have lost any proper understanding of risk. As long as tobacco is legal, people should be free to balance the pleasures and dangers themselves."

Daily Telegraph, 23 June 2005

"But here's old Ken – he's been crass, he's been insensitive and thuggish and brutal in his language – but I don't think actually if you read what he said, although it was extraordinary and rude, I don't think he was actually anti-Semitic."

The Times, 17 February 2005

"I realised I was being heckled by a blooming bishop, and from that moment on my speech was irretrievable."

"Ken [Livingstone] doesn't think he's got anything to say sorry for and if that's really his feeling, then I think that he should stick to his guns."

"Ok, I said to myself as I sighted the bird down the end of the gun. This time, my fine feathered friend, there is no escape."

Friends, Voters, Countrymen, p59.

"Howard is a dynamic performer on many levels. There you are. He sent me to Liverpool. Marvellous place. Howard was the most effective Home Secretary since Peel. Hang on, was Peel Home Secretary?"

On Michael Howard, *The Times*, 19 April 2005, p.23.

On driving an Alfa Romeo:

"She was blonde. She was beautiful. She was driving some poxy little Citroen or Peugeot thing... And she had just overtaken me... And let me tell you, I wasn't having it. Because if there is one thing calculated to make the testosterone slosh in your ears like the echoing sea and the red mist of war descend over your eyes, it's being treated as though you were an old woman by a young woman... the whole endocrine orchestra said: 'Go. Take.' You can't be dissed by some blonde in a 305."

"There is absolutely no one, apart from yourself, who can prevent you, in the middle of the night, from sneaking down to tidy up the edges of that hunk of cheese at the back of the fridge."

Daily Telegraph, 27 May 2004, on the dangers of obesity.

"What we hate, what we fear, is being ignored."

On the fears of MP's. 21 April 2005.

"I think they get a fair squeeze of the sauce bottle."

Questioned by Michael Crick on his dedication to his political career and the Conservative Party, 2005.

"It is utterly absurd that Labour should be calling on us all to remember the value of that inclusive word 'British', when it is the government's own devolution programme which has fomented the rising sense of Scottishness, and Englishness."

Lend Me Your Ears, p209

"I'm very attracted to it. I may be diverting from Tory Party policy here, but I don't care."

On 24 hour drinking legislation. Andrew Pierce, *The Times*, 30 April 2005.

"Will I throw my hat into the ring? It depends on what kind of ring it is and what kind of hat I have in my hand."

When asked by the *Oxford Mail* if he will stand for leader of the Conservative Party.

"The proposed ban on incitement to 'religious hatred' makes no sense unless it involves a ban on the Koran itself."

Daily Telegraph, 21 July 2005

"When is *Little Britain* going to do a sketch, starring Matt Lucas as one of the virgins? Islam will only be truly acculturated to our way of life when you could expect a Bradford audience to roll in the aisles at Monty Python's Life of Mohammed."

"Life isn't like coursework, baby. It's one damn essay crisis after another."

In an article titled 'Exams work because they're scary', *Daily Telegraph*, 12 May 2005.

"It is a wonder that the Dutch look so tall and healthy, when you consider what they eat."

Lend Me Your Ears, p19.

"I think I was once given cocaine but I sneezed so it didn't go up my nose. In fact, it may have been icing sugar."

Evening Standard, 17 October 2005, p.15.

"I'm a rugby player, really, and I knew I was going to get to him, and when he was about two yards away I just put my head down. There was no malice. I was going for the ball with my head, which I understand is a legitimate move in soccer."

On his tackle on German midfielder Maurizio Gaudino in a charity football match, May 2006.

"I love the skyline of New York, the city of my birth. There are few things more beautiful than the skyscrapers against the cold, bright blue sky. That skyline has now been changed by terror.

But buildings will rise on that site again; perhaps not as big as what was there before; perhaps, knowing the Americans, bigger. That is as it should be. To accept that the world is reshaped is to do the terrorists' work."

"He may seem like a lovable buffoon but you know he wouldn't hesitate to line you all up against a wall and have you shot."

Jeremy Hardy on Radio 4.

"There may be a reason I can't think of but the problem with that reason is that I can't think of it now."

"I love tennis with a passion. I challenged Boris Becker to a match once and he said he was up for it but he never called back. I bet I could make him run around."

The Express, 21 March 2005.

"If this is war, let's win it. Let's fly with whatever it takes to the mountain eyrie of Bin Laden, winkle him out, and put him on trial. If we can find good evidence that he is guilty, and he puts up any resistance, then let's not even bother with the judicial process. Let's find the scum who did this and wipe them off the face of the Earth."

"We should be careful, in the current climate, of rushing through legislation that goes too far in expanding the powers of the state. We should beware of eroding our freedoms, when freedom is what we are supposed to be fighting for. O Crime, what liberties are removed in thy name."

"The President is a cross-eyed Texan warmonger, unelected, inarticulate, who epitomises the arrogance of American foreign policy."

On George W Bush. Unsigned editorial entitled 'Infantile resentment' in *The Spectator*, 22 November 2003.

"He's the sort of person who 200 years ago would have died aged 30 leading a cavalry charge into a volcano."

Frankie Boyle on *Mock the Week*

"I've always known my life would be turned into a farce. I'm just glad its been entrusted to two such distinguished men of letters."

"Och aye, it's the New Jerusalem! It's a land of milk and honey they're building up there in Scotland, laddie. They'll nae be doing with your horrid Anglo-Saxon devil-take-the-hindmost approach. No, they're just more socialist than us sour-mouthed Sassenachs."

"It's economically illiterate. A degree in classics or philosophy can be as valuable as anything else."

"I have founded the Pie Liberation Front. Our campaign to smuggle traditional British food to schoolchildren begins next week. Will you be our honorary patron?"

"No one obeys the speed limit except a motorised rickshaw."

Daily Telegraph, 12 July 2001.

"You are a self-centred, pompous twit. Even your body language on TV is pathetic. Get out of public life. Go and do something in the private sector."

Paul Bigley (brother of murdered hostage, Kenneth Bigley) to Johnson on Radio City in Liverpool, 21 October 2004.

"I'm in charge here!"

When things on *Have I Got News For You* threatened to get out of hand.

> "The people of Liverpool are a crowd of mawkish whingers. Why did you apologise?"
>
> Jim Bernard, Manchester

"In the course of my inglorious pilgrimage of penitence I tried to distinguish between *The Spectator's* attack on a general culture of sentimentality and grievance – which I stood by – and some offensive errors of fact about Hillsborough, for which I grovelled."

"How can somebody as fat as you get so many good-looking women to find you attractive?"
Ardal Conyngham, Belfast

"This strikes me as a trap question."

"Have you ever taken illegal drugs? If not why not?"
Lois Beene, Cardiff

"I have and I want you to know that I inhaled. Then I sneezed."

"Do you ever harbour lustful thoughts about the honourable women members sitting opposite you on the House of Commons benches? If yes, which ones?"
Steve Cant, Hastings

"They are all perfectly lovely in their own ways. I am rather shocked that you should ask."

"You confessed to having had a crush on Polly Toynbee. What is it about Polly that seems to drive Tory boys wild?"
Tom Scarsdale, by e-mail

"Oh lord. It's just she's so bossy and posh. Is that the right answer?"

"Have the Ancient Romans anything to teach the Tories about power?"
Gabriella Kruse, Bristol

"Yeah – that it's easily lost to the Vandals."

"Who is your historical pin-up, and why?"
Amelia Lancaster, Derby

"Pericles. Look at his funeral speech. Democracy. Freedom. Champion stuff."

"Are education standards slipping in Britain?"

Richard Morris, Luton

"Slipping! How could you even suggest it? Every year, comrades, our children are getting better and better at passing exams! Every year we produce more A*-C grade tractors from the Red Star plant! This year an amazing 43.5 per cent of candidates got an A at maths A-level, and guess what the proportion was 40 years ago, when far fewer people took maths A-level? It was only 7 per cent! Now you do the maths. Oh, all right, I'll do it for you. That is a staggering 620 per cent improvement by our young geniuses. Let me enter the usual political guff about how hard everyone has worked, and let me congratulate them on their grades. But if too many CVs read like a man falling off a building then the A is useless as a tool of differentiation, and that is why some universities are calling for a pre-U exam to replace A-levels, and that is why there is increasing interest in the IB. We have all connived in the fiction that our kids are getting brighter, because that conceals the growing gulf in attainment between much of the maintained sector and the grammar schools/independent schools. The result is that the market has, inevitably, asserted itself, and in a way that is socially regressive. Which schools, after all, are going to have the resources to prepare their pupils for these new specialised university entrance exams?"

From *The Independent*, 2 January 2007

In an outstanding journalistic coup, *The Telegraph* acquired a copy of Boris's Mayoral application form. As you can imagine, it's not a boring dirge of sycophancy – in the "Challenge's faced" section, he writes:

1. Trying to help raise 4 children in inner London.
   Outcome: Too early to call, but looking promising.

2. Taking on Blair and Campbell in the battle of Black Rod's Memorandum on the Queen Mother's lying-in-state.
   Outcome: Total victory.

3. Negotiating Hyde Park Corner by bicycle.
   Outcome: Survival.

"I'm backing David Cameron's campaign out of pure, cynical self-interest."

On the 2005 Conservative leadership contest. *The Independent*, 5 October 2005.

"The other day I was giving a pretty feeble speech when it went off the cliff and became truly abysmal. It was at some kind of founder's dinner for a university, and I had badly miscalculated my audience. I thought it was going to be a bunch of students, and when I saw the elite group of retired generals, former *Telegraph* editors and Nobel Prize-winning economists, all in black tie, with their wives, I desperately tried to extemporise something profound. There were some musty sepulchres set into the wall of the ancient hall, so I started burbling about social mobility in the 18th century and widening participation in universities today. Frankly, I thought my sermon was more or less ideal. I began some guff-filled sentence with the words, 'I am sure we all agree...' It seemed to go well, so I did it again. 'I am sure we all agree we need world-class skills...', I said, or something equally banal, at which point a man down the table shot to his feet and shouted, 'Well, I don't! I don't agree with what you are saying at all. It seems to me to be quite wrong for you to claim that we all agree when I don't agree.' And blow me down, he appeared to be wearing long purple vestments. It was, of course, Britain's most turbulent priest, the Bishop of Southwark. I realised I was being heckled by a blooming bishop, and from that moment on my speech was irretrievable. I told a long and rambling story about sheep, in the hope that the man of God would be appeased, and sat down. I did sniff him later on, and though there was an aroma of hot cassock he didn't seem notably drunk."

From *The Spectator*, 27th January 2007

"Vote Johnson, vote often — there is a ready supply of Johnsons waiting to step into whatever breaches are left in whatever constituencies."

Boris while out visiting his dad's Teignbridge constituency.

"I will never vote to ban hunting. It is a piece of spite that has nothing to do with animal welfare, and everything to do with Blair's manipulation of rank-and-file Labour chippiness and class hatred."

Friends, Voters, Countrymen, p146

"I got to page 1264 of *War and Peace*. It was really hotting up, but unfortunately I lost my copy."

"I have as much chance of becoming Prime Minister as of being decapitated by a frisbee or of finding Elvis."

Daily Mail, 22 July 2003

"Devolution is causing all the strains that its opponents predicted, and in allowing the Scots to make their own laws, while free-riding on English taxpayers, it is simply unjust. The time will come when the Scots will discover that their personal care for the elderly is too expensive, and they will come, cap in hand to Uncle Sugar in London. And when they do, I propose that we tell them to hop it."

"What I would advise fans is to expect little and possibly they'll receive even less."

Commenting on England vs Germany Legends match, 3rd May 2006.

"There is no finer subject. I say that without prejudice to other subjects, which you can basically read in your bath."

On the subject of classics, 2005.

"Statistically, I am due to be fired again."

When asked if he was due to be included in the latest Tory reshuffle, June 2007.

"Celebrating. I do think there's every chance. There's a swing on."

When asked what he will be doing the day after the election, 2005.

"We will demonstrate that we are the party that cares about the older generation by propelling a man who is so full of vim he will give me a thrashing on the squash court and has nine-and-a-half grandchildren."

Trying to get his dad elected in Teignbridge, 2005.

[I have been propelled] "as a fat German tourist may be transported by superior alpinists to the summit of Everest."

Praising colleagues at *The Spectator* in his leaving speech, December 2005.

"The whole point about representative democracy is not that it is perfectly representative of the views of the people, but that the representatives should do their duty by their consciences."

"It may be that the psychological effort needed to haul myself around into a more gaffe-free zone proves too difficult."

When asked if he was due to be included in the latest Tory reshuffle, June 2007.

"I have successfully ridden two horses for quite a long time. But I have to admit there have been moments when the distance between the two horses has grown terrifyingly wide, and I did momentarily come off."

Boris reflecting on his very public 2004 downfall, November 2005.

"Among the many reasons for mourning the passing of Auberon Waugh is that he will not be here to witness the final obliteration of hunting by the Labour Party... If I were not a Tory, I think I would become one on this issue alone."

Daily Telegraph, 18 January 2001.

"I'm having Sunday lunch with my family. I'm vigorously campaigning, inculcating my children in the benefits of a Tory government."

Asked whether he was canvassing at Sunday lunchtime, *The Guardian*, 11 April 2005.

"It is time for concerted cultural imperialism. They are wrong about women. We are right. We can't have them blowing us up. The deluded fanatics must be helped to a more generous understanding of the world. Female education is the answer to the global population problem. It is the ultimate answer to the problem of Islamic fundamentalist terrorism."

"All politicians in the end are like crazed wasps in a jam jar, each individually convinced that they are going to make it."

On his political ambitions, November 2005.

"I've got my fingers in several dykes."

Conservative Party Conference, 6 October 2004.

"Their policy on cake is pro-having it and pro-eating it."

Discussing Liberal Democrat policies.

"The royal family are living memorials, the history of the country written in their DNA, a bit like the inscriptions on the Menin Gate. Unlike the Menin Gate, thanks to human reproduction, those genes can go on for ever."

"My hair has yet to induce epilepsy and cost considerably less than £400,000 to design."

When Boris's hair was compared to the new London 2012 Olympic logo, 9 June 2007.

"Ich bin ein Frankfurter."

Uttered while discussing educational freedom (derived from Felix Frankfurter).

"We are still the second most important country on Earth. The trick of maintaining such influence, of course, is to go around pretending to be very bumbling and hopeless and self-deprecating, a skill at which we excel."

"Now, there will be plenty of British Conservatives who think these Taliban chappies run a tight ship, women's lib is not an unalloyed blessing, look at all these poofters these days, and so on. There are even ex-feminists, such as Germaine Greer, who will take a perverse pleasure in announcing that women can look very beautiful in a veil."

"I have not had an affair with Petronella. It is complete balderdash. It is an inverted pyramid of piffle. It is all completely untrue and ludicrous conjecture. I am amazed people can write this drivel."

Denying accusations of his having an affair with Petronella Wyatt. *Mail on Sunday*, 7 November 2004.

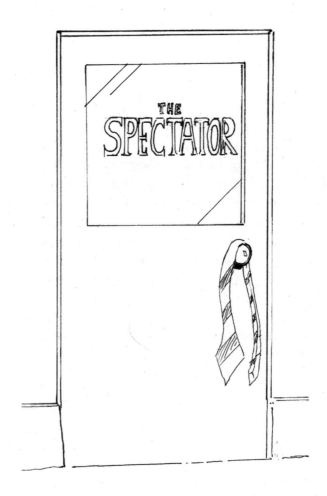

"If the fuel strikers had not struck, people would never have grasped so clearly how much money Gordon is filching. It is thanks to the fuel protesters that we understand what a regressive tax it is, and how it has helped the tax burden of the poorest fifth of society to rise by three per cent since 1997. It is thanks to the fuel strikers that tax and public spending are now again at the centre of politics. Blair will say he can't cut taxes because it is inflationary, or because he needs to spend the money on pensions, or schools or hospitals. He can't have it both ways."

"My ambition silicon chip has been programmed to try to scramble up this ladder, so I do feel a kind of sense that I have got to."

Describing his political ambitions, November 2005.

"Hello, I'm your MP. Actually I'm not. I'm your candidate. Gosh."

Canvassing in Henley, 2005.

"It is often immigrants who like waving flags and receiving CBEs, and they certainly seem pretty good at cricket."

Discussing the pros and cons of British immigration.

"The trouble with campaigning in the wilds of Oxfordshire is that you lose touch with the main battle. I feel lost in the jungle, way up the Nong River, 75 clicks beyond the Do Long bridge."

"I'm like a greased panther, a coiled spring, all that suppressed kinetic energy."

Commenting on England vs Germany Legends match, 3rd May 2006.

"Maybe the Tories would do better, and be in a position to act Right, if they began by talking Left, by explaining the minimal Tory view of the state and society. Because no one looking at the Thatcherites' spending record could be in any doubt: those people thought there was such a thing as society."

"One man's Mickey Mouse course is another man's literae humaniores."

Discussing the "lite" courses studied at British universities.

"That is the best case for Bush; that, among other things, he liberated Iraq. It is good enough for me."

Daily Telegraph, 26 February 2004.

"I'd want to get Blair and really interrogate the guy. I'd really want to pin him up against a palm tree and slap him around and get the truth out of him about a few things we need a bit of elucidation."

"You know, whenever George Dubya Bush appears on television, with his buzzard squint and his Ronald Reagan side-nod, I find a cheer rising irresistibly in my throat. Yo, Bush baby, I find myself saying, squashing my beer can like some crazed red-neck. You tell 'em boy. Just you tell all those pointy-headed liberals where to get off."

Lend me Your Ears, p317

"This is the Government that promised to build a 'New Britain', that told us that 'things could only get better', and what was their salient commitment to the nation yesterday, apart from some hoary old bilge about drunken yobbery? It was to pick on a small group of a few thousand eccentrics who like to potter around the countryside on their horses, endlessly breaking their collarbones, and to tell them that whatever they're doing, they mustn't. This is government of the fox, for the fox, by the fox."

"We need an alternative, and one that doesn't just involve crucifying our landscape with wind farms which, even when they are in motion, would barely pull the skin of a rice pudding."

Have I Got Views For You, p83

"There is no need here to rehearse the steps of matricide. Howe pounced, Heseltine did his stuff. After it was all over, my wife, Marina, claimed she came upon me, stumbling down a street in Brussels, tears in my eyes, and claiming that it was as if someone had shot Nanny."

Lend Me Your Ears, p13

"I am far too terrified to dissent from the growing world creed of global warming."

"Give that man a handbag! And while you're at it, tell him to wear a powder blue suit and a pineapple coloured wig next time he wants to impersonate this century's greatest peace time Prime Minister."

Lend Me Your Ears, p132

"Mrs Thatcher pioneered a revolution that was imitated in one way or another, around the world."

Lend Me Your Ears, p134

"It [the 'Building and Buildings, England and Wales' regulation] is the 4,633rd regulation the Government has introduced this year. If this Government has any architectural legacy whatsoever, apart from the Dome, it will be a host of yawning unrepaired windows. It is through one of those apertures that they should chuck these and other regulations, before it is too late."

"It's time they were ejected into outer space."

On the Labour Party, 2005.

"There are not many Lib Dems in Parliament, but even in that tiny group they incarnate dozens of diametrically opposing positions. You want to know what the Lib Dem policy is on taxation, for instance, and you want to know whether you are for or against a 50 per cent tax rate. One half of your cerebrum thinks it quite right that the rich should pay more; the other lobe thinks tax is quite high enough already. You are a perfect Lib Dem, a mass of contradictions, and your party supplies exactly what you are looking for."

Have I Got Views For You, p90.

"We seem to have forgotten that societies need rich people, even sickeningly rich people, and not just to provide jobs for those who clean swimming pools and resurface tennis courts."

Lend Me Your Ears, p384

"When you see a mugging on Holloway Road, and the villain scarpers into the night, there's no point looking around for a policeman. But in due course the police turn up in a high-powered car, and you are ferried with flashing lights, up and down, up and down – in a macho Starsky and Hutch display that has become utterly banal – while the mugger has melted away."

[On test driving a Nissan Murano] "Tee hee," I said to myself as I took in the ludicrously arrogant Darth Vader-style snout. What was it saying, with the plutocratic sneer of that gleaming grille?

It was saying "out of my way, small car driven by ordinary person on modest income. Make way for Murano!"

Life in the Fast Lane, p239

"If we Tories wished to reverse just one year's growth in Whitehall, we would have to sack the equivalent of the entire population of Ilfracombe, the seaside town in Devon!"

"I was at this party in Islington the other day and we were all glugging back the champagne, and suddenly I could resist it no longer. The urge rose within me, as though some genie had seized the diaphragm. 'Hague,' I roared. 'Haguey! Don't you think he's absolutely right to say this stuff about crime? Isn't he spot on?' And their eyes bulged like the very crustaceans on the canapes."

"We should never forget that in asking people to vote for us we are essentially asking to take charge of taxation and spending, and that our prime duty is to bring a new and more sensible – and more Conservative – style of economic management... the public sector is continuing to expand, and Brown is taking ever more money from the private sector to fund this expansion, and therefore preventing its use in wealth creation or the generation of new jobs."

Have I Got Views For You, p95

"Terrible outbreak of afternoon kipping in Henley. Always in their dressing gowns, hard at it."

On the police:

"A cynic would say that they were all stuck on racial awareness programmes; or deployed in desperate attempts to catch paedophiles in ancient public schools; or lurking in lay-bys in the hope of penalising a motorist; or perhaps preparing for the great moment when they will be able to arrest anyone who allows his dogs to chase rabbits, let alone those who go foxhunting."

"You can continue to believe in the NHS as the sole and sufficient provider... or you can conclude that this is one of the reasons why we have a system which treats the patients as dolts and serfs..."

"The chief constables originally had good reasons for thinking that it was a waste of manpower to have men in uniform pounding the pavements, or cycling through tranquil villages. Their men were likely to stumble across a robbery in progress, on average, once every eight years. What the chiefs forgot is the psychological effect of denuding the streets of coppers. There is a sense of lawlessness around, and insolent impunity. As for those policemen who are still on the beat, they have plenty of excuse for feeling assailed by this Government."

"Hunting is crucial to Labour, because it gives some contour to the semolina-like blob of Tony Blair's ideology. For the millions of Labour voters who have been depressed by the Government's failures in the public services, it is one of the few overt chances they will get for class warfare; and conversely the quarrel over hunting enables Labour ministers to caricature their opponents as tweed-wearing Waugh-reading defenders of atavism."

"We can be as nice as pie, we can take our ties off and breakdance down the esplanade and all wear earrings and all the rest of it. It won't make any difference to the electorate if they don't think we're going to offer a new and improved, basically Conservative approach to government."

Conservative Conference, 2005

Boris Factfile

. . . .

Boris Johnson is a Euro-sceptic, British right-wing journalist and Conservative Member of Parliament.

Full Name: Alexander Boris de Pfeffel Johnson

Born: New York, 19th June 1964

Siblings: Leo, Rachel, Jo

Education: Eton, before studying Classics at Balliol College, Oxford

Married: Marina Wheeler in 1993

Children: Milo, Theo, Laura, Cassia

Career:

1983 - President of the Oxford Union

1987 - Trainee reporter for *The Times*

1987 - Reporter for the *Wolverhampton Express and Star*

1987 - Leader and feature writer at *The Daily Telegraph*

1989 - Became European Community correspondent for *The Daily Telegraph*

1994 - Assistant Editor for *The Daily Telegraph*

1994 - Political columnist for *The Spectator* (1 year)

1997 - Unsuccessful in becoming Member of Parliament for Clwyd South

1999 - Became Editor of *The Spectator*

2001 - Became Member of Parliament for Henley-on-Thames

2003 - Became Vice-Chairman of the Conservative Party

2004 - Appointed Shadow Minister for the Arts

2004 - Nominated in 2004 for a BAFTA television award

2004 - Sacked as Minister of Arts after allegations of adulterous affair

2005 - December - Resigned from Spectator editorship to take up position as Shadow Minister for Higher Education

2007 - Announces candidacy for the Conservative nomination for London Mayor. Resigns his position as Shadow Minister for Higher Education

Other notable facts:

- Boris has spoken in **16 debates** in the last year — below average amongst MPs.

- Boris has received answers to **136 written questions** in the last year — well above average amongst MPs.

- He replied within 2 or 3 weeks to **a high** number of messages sent via WriteToThem.com during 2006, according to constituents.

- Boris gas voted in **52% of votes** in parliament — well below average amongst MPs. (From Public Whip.)

- Boris's speeches are understandable to an average **17-18** year old, going by the **Flesch-Kincaid Grade Level** score.

- Boris has used three-word alliterative phrases (e.g. "she sells seashells") **112 times** in debates — average amongst MPs.

How Boris Votes in Parliament:

- Has **never voted** on a **transparent Parliament**

- Voted **moderately against** introducing a **smoking ban**

- Voted **moderately against** introducing **ID cards**

- Voted **strongly against** introducing **foundation hospitals**

- Voted **strongly against** introducing **student top-up fees**

- Voted **moderately against** Labour's **anti-terrorism laws**

- Voted **very strongly** for the **Iraq war**

- Voted **strongly for** investigating the **Iraq war**

- Voted **very strongly for** replacing **Trident**

- Voted **very strongly against** the **foxhunting ban**

- Voted **a mixture of for and against** equal **gay rights**

Miscellaneous Boris:

- Boris has appeared **four** times on *Have I Got News For You*, three times as guest presenter.

- Boris currently commands **12,793** majority in Henley-on-Thames, the 151st safest seat in the country.

- In this Parliament he has reb elled against the Conservative whip **twice** – on animal rights and terrorism.

- Boris has a voting record of **51.9%** in this session of Parliament.

- He has spoken in Parliament **35** times in the past year, as well as submitting **27** written questions.

- He replies to **72%** of messages sent via FaxYourMP.com within 14 days.

- Boris has attended **57%** of votes in Parliament.

Courtesy of Boris Watch www.boriswatch.com, Theyworkforyou.com, Publicwhip.org, FaxYourMP.com

The Boris Bibliography:

- *Friends, Voters, Countrymen*, HarperCollins, 2001
- *Lend Me Your Ears*, HarperCollins, 2003
- *Have I Got Views For You*, HarperCollins, 2006
- *Seventy-Two Virgins*, HarperCollins, 2004
- The *Dream of Rome*, HarperCollins, 2005
- *Life in the Fast Lane*, HarperCollins, 2007
- *Perils of the Pushy Parents*, HarperCollins, 2007 (forthcoming)
- *The British*, HarperCollins, 2008 (forthcoming)

Boris on the Web:

- Offical Blog www.boris-johnson.com
- Boris Watch www.boriswatch.com
- Boris Mayoral Campaign www.backboris.com

By others:

Boris: *The Rise of Boris Johnson* by Andrew Gimson, Pocket Books, 2006